CATCH THAT PESKY THOUGHT!

BLOOMSBURY EDUCATION

Bloomsbury Publishing Plc
50 Bedford Square, London WC1B 3DP, UK

Bloomsbury Publishing Ireland Limited
29 Earlsfort Terrace, Dublin 2, D02 AY28, Ireland

First published in Great Britain, 2026 by Bloomsbury Publishing Plc

A catalogue record for this book is available from the British Library

ISBN: PB: 978-1-80199-813-0; ePub: 978-1-80199-812-3

2 4 6 8 10 9 7 5 3 1

Printed and bound in China by C&C Offset Printing Co., Ltd., Shenzhen, Guangdong

To find out more about our authors and books visit www.bloomsbury.com and sign up for our newsletters

For product safety related questions contact productsafety@bloomsbury.com

CATCH THAT PESKY THOUGHT!

BLOOMSBURY EDUCATION
LONDON OXFORD NEW YORK NEW DELHI SYDNEY

From Boston to Buenos Aires,
from Taiwan to Tangier,
you'll find some cheeky creatures,
whispering mischief in your ear.

Watch out, you won't see them coming,
they're masters of stealth and disguise.
At the top of the World's 'Most Wanted' list,
behold with your very own eyes...

THE PESKIES!

A Pesky is the **NAUGHTIEST** pixie.
It's **SNEAKY** and **RASCALLY RUDE.**

Like a thief it creeps in with a dastardly grin
to trick you and steal your good mood!

Jenrola had built up her courage
to ask if she could play.
When a Pesky thought popped into her head,
and told her to run away...

Harry was trying his hardest,
learning how to write.
When a Pesky thought crept into his mind,
that he'd **NEVER** get it right...

Neve had been practising daily,
her lines for the school summer show.
But when it was time to stand up and speak,
the worrying thoughts wouldn't go...

Leon dreamed of being an astronaut,
the first kid to land on Mars.
But the Pesky thoughts came rocketing in,
when his spaceship fell short of the stars...

At lunchtime, the friends were all silent,
filled with thoughts they believed were their own.

I'm **RUBBISH**, I'm **STUPID**, I'm the **WORST** in the world,
NO-ONE likes me, I'm **ALWAYS** alone.

The children looked up at each other,
feeling as if they might cry,
when a tiny mouse with a gigantic net
came **CRASHING** down out of the sky...

'WHACK!' went the net on the table,
launching fish and chips in the air.
With eyes like saucers and mouths open wide,
they gawked at the mouse landing there.

WHAAAAAAAAAAACK!!!!

'BAMBOOZLED!' yelled the mouse as he wrestled his net.
'Bam... what?' asked the children, surprised.

'BAMBOOZLED! FOOLED! My friends, you've been **TRICKED** by those hoodwinking thieves in disguise!'

The friends gathered round while the mouse explained:

but you're **NOT** the worst, **NOT** rubbish, **NOT** alone!

'CATCH THAT PESKY THOUGHT!'

The way to spot a Pesky thought
is to catch how it speaks to you.
Is it full of unkind and negative words,
that are powerful but simply **NOT TRUE?!**

Words like...

are clues that it might be a trick.
If you think that a Pesky is trying its luck,
then **CATCH THAT THOUGHT,** challenge it, quick!

Jenrola ran off whooping,
and returned with a box full of scraps.
'Come on team!' she giggled.
'Let's build some **PESKY TRAPS!**'

THE GLUE GRIP
THE WEBJAILER
THE TRICKSY TRAMPOLINE

And now my friends, here's the fun part,
either those Pesky thoughts can stay,
or **YOU** can **CHOOSE** to send them right back
and not let them **RUIN** your day!

Take this Pesky thought with you!

PESKY THOUGHT

ALWAYS
NEVER
CAN'T
BYE BYE!

So next time your confidence wobbles
and a Pesky thought sneaks its way through,
remember that **YOU** hold the **POWER**
to catch it and challenge it too!

CATCH THAT

PESKY THOUGHT!

WELCOME TO...

THE COURAGE CLUB

This story is part of **The Courage Club** series – helping children (and their adults!) build bravery, take risks, and go after hard things together.

The bigger picture

So much of our approach to mental health is reactive: we wait until there's a problem before stepping in to 'fix' it. At *The Courage Club* we believe in a more proactive approach - one that supports ALL children to build strong emotional foundations right from the start. This is not just to equip children with the tools to cope when life's challenges come but also to empower them with the skills to thrive well beyond that.

The Courage Club is built around three core strands of child development:

I CAN

Character:
how I engage with my world

I AM

Self-Esteem:
how I see myself

I WILL

Resilience:
how I respond to challenges

Where this Story fits

Catch That Pesky Thought! helps children see that not every thought that pops into their head is true – and that we can choose which ones we listen to. Those sneaky, negative thoughts that say, 'You're not good enough' or 'You can't do it' can feel powerful, but they don't have to be in charge. By turning the process into a fun, playful game – 'Catch that pesky thought!' – children learn to spot unhelpful thinking and challenge it. When adults model this too, we help children build the confidence to take charge of their thinking and not be bossed around by pesky, negative thoughts.

So, let's keep saying it out loud, together: